BONE DANCE

Volume 27

SUN TRACKS

An American Indian

Literary Series

Series Editor

Ofelia Zepeda

Editorial Committee

Vine Deloria, Jr.

Larry Evers

Joy Harjo

N. Scott Momaday

Emory Sekaquaptewa

Leslie Marmon Silko

BONE
DANCE

NEW AND
SELECTED
POEMS
1965-1993

WENDY
ROSE

THE UNIVERSITY
OF ARIZONA PRESS

TUCSON & LONDON

The University of Arizona Press

Copyright © 1994 Arizona Board of Regents

All Rights Reserved

⊛ This book is printed on acid-free, archival-quality paper.
Manufactured in the United States of America

98 97 96 95 94   6 5 4 3 2 1

Library of Congress Cataloging-in-Publication Data

Rose, Wendy.
    Bone dance : new and selected poems, 1965–1993 / Wendy Rose.
       p.   cm. — (Sun tracks ; v. 27)
       ISBN 0–8165–1412–7 (acid-free paper). — ISBN 0–8165–1428–3
    (pbk. : acid-free paper)
       1. Indians of North America—Poetry. I. Title. II. Series.
    PS3568.07644B66   1994
    811'.54—dc 20   93–21117
                                                                        CIP

British Library Cataloguing-in-Publication Data

A catalogue record for this book is available.

Publication of this book is made possible in part by a grant from
the Arizona Commission on the Arts through appropriations from the
Arizona State Legislature and grants from the National Endowment
for the Arts.

Contents

Introduction

Early spring mornings in Coarsegold can fool you. Yesterday, for instance, I enjoyed increasingly white-hot sun for the first part of the day, and fussed over the cacti with whom I share a particularly funky farmhouse *sans* farm. By late afternoon, swirls of high clouds began to spread into the San Joaquin Valley, two thousand feet below me, and thunderheads raised their huge fists from behind the Sierra Nevada in whose foothills I live. The wind came up and the temperature dropped until, by midnight, it was only eight degrees above freezing. Now, as I write this, the cacti again relax in the early morning sun, though I suppose they don't really trust it anymore. The very tender plants, from rain forest rather than desert, have been brought indoors to spend the night with their human companion.

It is not a casual thing, that I live in Coarsegold. I am only thirty-five miles from Mariposa, the county seat in which or near various ancestors lived. My maternal grandmother left Mariposa as a young woman around the turn-of-the-century and settled in Berkeley to raise her family with her English husband. I feel certain ancestors here very strongly, both immigrant and native. I know a few names, a few histories, but only feel some of the others. I know about Margaret on the wagon train from Missouri in the early 1850s, who bought her house in Bear Valley from John C. Fremont and managed the Bon Ton Saloon. And I know Margaret's husband Maurice, the Prussian draft dodger. I know about Joseph, born in an Irish castle, who earned and lost a small fortune in gold after 1849, one of a few lucky miners but not so well-endowed with wisdom, and his wife, Henrietta, whose

Scottish father had been raised by Sir Walter Scott. And, of course, there are the muted voices that I have always heard, Miwok ghosts who remain around the redbud branches, following the Merced River to the sea and back, as they search for what they are searching for. I am the first generation to return to these hills, and I didn't even set out to do it. It just happened. That is, of course, if anything ever just happens.

My father's people, too, fastened still to their fields and mesas in northern Arizona, have something to do with these poems. The tough stocky corn is as much a part of me as the acorn baskets and books. Perhaps it is that part which refuses to stay dead and instead emerges each year to reenact that original Emergence. Perhaps that is the part insisting that if the words cannot be sung in the genuine language of the old way, that they be written instead. Too city-stupid to know any better, I am left with the paper and pen for my magic.

About the age of eighteen or twenty, I thought that people like me were supposed to become buffers between the Elders and the invasion forces (in whatever form they should take, be it armed with guns or holding government documents). I actually thought that I had to be strong, with the thousands of others like me in my generation, so that the fragile, old knowledge would be protected. At forty-five, I see things a little differently. I had it the wrong way around. It is the old way of remembering the teachings and performing the ceremonies that is strong, while people like me are the ones who have always been in danger. I learned that my true job is to simply be who I am and keep listening. I know I will never be an Elder, never able to live on the earth as a traditional Hopi woman on Hopi land, or hear the voices in their own language and understand them. It is too late for that and it has always been too late. Without a Hopi mother, I am not even part of a clan. Learning all of this had a great deal to do with my writing of poetry. How can you hope to speak if you have no voice? Neither cast-offs, nor mongrels, nor assimilated sellouts, nor traditionalists, those who are like me are fulfilling in our own way a certain level of existence, a pattern in the prophecy. We must be here, though we cannot be soldiers or shields for those who are so much stronger than we are. We merely face the same enemy.

Why does the daughter of natives and strangers, gold miners and ranchers, write poetry? I can only mark certain times in my life when writing poetry was really the logical thing to do. For instance, there was a time when what I knew could have burst from inside of me in other ways. The first poem that I ever wrote, consciously knowing that it was a poem, was when I heard on the radio the news about the church bombing in Birmingham. I remember that I had the flu and felt something so enormous that it had to spill out somehow. About that same time, I began to feel connected to "a People" for the first time, in spite of having grown up in the Bay Area attending Catholic school. Of course, I didn't yet know "the People" have something to say about whether or not you are one of them. I began to write about what I was learning in my urban Indian community in Oakland and San Francisco. I began to identify so thoroughly and personally with whoever was facing injustice in Indian Country, that I felt Kinzua Dam* drown me, and Termination** invalidate my identity, and two-hundred-year-old treaties break across my bones. In the first section of this volume, *Hopi Roadrunner Dancing*, I have included "For My People" (which was in that small book) with several others written before 1973. The second poem, "The Long Root" was written on the day the United States began its air attacks on Cambodia. The third poem, "Mano," was the surreal experience of walking the streets of Berkeley carefully picking my way around rubble and broken glass, and won-

---

*Kinzua Dam in Pennsylvania flooded Seneca land that had been guaranteed protection in a treaty bearing Washington's signature.

**Termination is the unilateral congressional act of ending the federal government's trust obligation to the Native governments.

dering how people living in such a place find food, or water, or become strong when the environment has been shattered. The last poem, "Lab Genesis," focuses on my first years in college, during the mid-1960s, when my classes in archaeology caused a crisis. It seems that I could *feel* the trowels, *feel* my bones smother in paper bags in a lab, *become* extinct in a museum display. Rather than peering down into the excavated pit, I found that I was, instead, staring up at the archaeologist from below.

The second section is from *Long Division: A Tribal History*. These poems were written from the perspective of someone discovering that writing poetry was something she could do. When I was eighteen, an English instructor told me that I had "a flair" for writing. I wasn't sure what to do with that information, but a few years later met Maurice Kenny in a San Francisco cabaret where we sat listening to one of the "whiteshaman"* poets. Maurice says that I nearly caved in his ribs with my elbow—not too polite for our first meeting. I remember something more like banging on the table in disbelief at what I was hearing from a white man with a crude mask on his face from which hung a raccoon tail. That evening proved fruitful, not only in the publications by and with Maurice that have happened since, but also in the friendship that endures to this day. If these poems are pretentious, as in referring to myself as "the Poet," it is only because I was catching a glimpse of my face in the mirror and discovering that I was a person.

In *Lost Copper*, my first large collection, I felt as if I were being presented, finally, to the sun and was no more than twenty days old.** Perhaps because the Malki Museum Press is on the Morongo Indian Reservation in southern California, or because of the delight in my growing relationship with Arthur Murata, or maybe for no special rea-

---

*"Whiteshaman" is a term coined by Geary Hobson to refer to non-Indians who assume a literary "shaman" persona to which they are not entitled.

**Hopi custom: 20-day-old baby is presented to the sun following confinement.

son at all, I began to feel that I was growing closer to a security I could not yet name. I recall that I learned something of the art of subtlety at that time. I learned not to tell the listener or reader what to feel through bombarding her or him with my feelings, but to allow the emotions and ironies to rush from her or his own heart on being presented with something that had greatly moved me. To do this requires encouraging the listener to be in the same place, to see what I see. I never felt that it was enough to display agility with words or clever turns of phrase. I believe that inaccessible poetry does not work. If the listener must take a special class in how to appreciate it (or any other form of art), then the poem has failed. I hold myself to that standard and try to remember that "ordinary" language contains all of the imagery and beauty needed by the poem.

During the late 1970s I began to write poems about traveling—partly because I couldn't afford other sorts of souvenirs, and partly because being able to travel so far from home was new and exciting. Before 1978 I had never been east of the Rocky Mountains. *What Happened When the Hopi Hit New York* is a collection of these poems, starting in California and ending up in New York City by a rather circuitous route through Alaska and New Orleans. There were a few high points during my first trip to New York City that I felt deserved to become souvenirs to savor later in life, such as the time I mistook the subway beneath an apartment building for a small earthquake, or how I took a suitcase full of food in case I couldn't find any in New York. I soon graduated, of course, to taking an empty suitcase in which to stuff fresh, hot New York bagels for the return trip to California.

As my travels increased and I began to see a little more of the world and its people on their home turf, I felt more and more a sense of being linked not only to Native American issues, but to related concerns on a global level. It has not surprised me that other Indian women writers went through a similar transformation at the same time, although I'm not sure why that is not surprising. In exploring what it means to be a "halfbreed," I learned that this is not a condition of genetics and has nothing to do with ancestry or race. Instead, "half-breedness" is a condition of history, a result of experience, of dislocations and reunions, and of choices made for better or worse. I began to study the lives of individuals who, for reasons I didn't know, profoundly affected me. All were victims of their place in history in some way. All were colonized souls. *The Halfbreed Chronicles* emerged from listening to those voices. In an emotional sense, I felt myself become Loo-Wit dislodging the resorts and loggers from her back, and Truganinny begging her younger relatives not to let the British Museum stuff her body and put her on display as the "Last Tasmanian," and the Salvadoran Native woman wandering in shock through her destroyed village and releasing her grief to a North American journalist, and Julia believing the words of her husband even as he plotted to profit at her expense. I, too, feel much like "the ugliest woman in the world" at times. I even "became" Robert Oppenheimer, my mother's one-time neighbor across the street in Berkeley, whose own choices laid the foundation for the death of hundreds of thousands of Japanese civilians and perhaps, someday, of the earth itself. In retrospect, I also have to take note of the fact that many of these "halfbreeds" did not survive the event that defined them, while others have endured or are still caught up in the whirlwind of their fate.

Maurice Kenny, a well-known Mohawk poet, and I have an ongoing argument conducted over coffee and hardrolls, about whether or not there are real mountains in the eastern part of North America. It seems that one day as we were driving in a rented car to New Hampshire from New York City, he kindly pointed out the Berkshires for me, clearly visible on the horizon. All I could see were some medium-sized sand dunes, so I asked "Where?" That started the argument and a collaboration with Maurice, *What the Mohawk Made the Hopi Say*, followed a few years later. We took the train from Washington, D.C. to New York City, and the bus from there to Akwesasne (Mohawk Nation) on the Canadian border. Part of the journey took us through the Adirondacks in the absolute dead of winter and, pressured by the thick ice forming on the inside of the bus windows, I admitted that the Adirondacks did appear to resemble mountains. Today Maurice makes his home in those beautiful soft mountains, just as I have moved into the sharp gray granite of the Sierra Nevada. The high point of my journey with Maurice into the Mohawk Nation was the tour of the Six Nations Museum in Onchiota in the middle of the night by a flashlight held by Ray Fadden (it is closed during the winter). I recall the power in the long belt of wampum lining the walls near the ceiling and I recall the boots I wore with ordinary socks in the twenty-below night.

In one way or another, while never as a leader, I have been involved with the "Indian Movement" since 1958, at the time a child observing and listening. I spent time, as we say, on Alcatraz after the prison closed and Bay Area Native people had occupied it, and have participated at some level in almost all of the events that have taken place during the 1960s to the present. In a genuine sense, I have offered my voice to the Movement, after all, it's the only thing I have to offer. I see no more important movement than that of indigenous people and their supporters around the earth, whether it is called "Green," "Aboriginal," or just, "Peoples." I have often been identified as a "protest poet" and, although something in me frowns a little at being so neatly categorized, it is largely the truth. There are those who think that Literature (capital L) must never be topical or personal, but rational and descriptive. It would never do for "art" to be useful. I don't believe that. What force could be more powerful than people moving together with a single voice? What could be more important and life-affirming than the unique-universal poetry of life itself? In *Going to War with All My Relations*, I selected poems that directly and self-consciously struggle with Movement issues. Some of the poems refer to events in which I took part or remember that have become history. Because the personal is political, as well, there are also a few poems in that volume of a less topical nature.

The final section of this volume, *Now Poof She Is Gone*, is made up mostly of unpublished poems, although some of them have been collected into a manuscript of the same title that is forthcoming.* These poems deal with the issues of personal crisis, dissolution and resolution, survival. Many of us in our middle years have found that our childhood terrors and mistreatments may lie buried during our early adult years, but eventually, as one therapist explained to me, "they come back around and bite you in the butt." Those of us who are female and have grown up in a culture that inexplicably views women as weaker versions of men rather than as the special strength that produces and nurtures life itself, have experienced a certain lack of willingness on the part of the literary world to acknowledge the importance of their issues. Women who have written from the "ouch" perspective have been dismissed all too often as invalid because they have "failed" to abstractly speak of "great themes" and to have used "great styles" in their Literature (capital L again). It is also true that "importance" and literary validity have been defined narrowly by a power structure that seeks to exclude the nitty-gritty of women's lives in much the same way as a colonial power seeks to silence the natives. They who own the publishers own the reviews own the bookstores own the universities. It is hardly surprising that "women's literature" is dismissed in much the same way as "ethnic literature." If we had been fortunate enough to spend some portion of our lives in our indigenous cultures, where power and access to it are structured very differently, we would not have suffered in silence for so long, unable to get our tongues around the gags that silence us. But many of us, perhaps most of us, live in a culture that has managed somehow to link "power" to the ability to destroy and these both to the phallus.

Now Poof She Is Gone (Firebrand Press, forthcoming)

Knowing that true masculinity is not that way and that such behaviors are very conscious political choices made by the leaders of colonizing cultures, I offer these "personal" poems to women and men in the spirit of conversation, exchange, and intimacy.

In an air-conditioned office in Fresno, I cannot feel at this moment what my cacti know. In another month or so, the days will be so hot that new growth may be scorched and it will be my responsibility to protect the tender green skin and spines from direct sun.

Coarsegold/Fresno
April 1993

HOPI
ROADRUNNER
DANCING

I was myself blown
two leafs apart
seeing the ground swim within
sliding and slipping together
and apart   .

growing closer
biting at our shadows
loving on our feet
dying in our souls
losing one another
losing ourselves

finding

Berkeley, 1965

THE LONG ROOT

(for Clif)

The feeling of sand in my eye
has somehow shortened my breath

allowed the night to descend
in its slow and twisting stream.

Voices disguise themselves,
plane smooth from me splinters

as I spread my bones on the mesa
so that part of me still believes

I will not be left here to die.
Before the intensity of summer

is that devastating storm
and no matter how I try

there is no way to shake
Cambodia from my Wounded Knee.

San Pablo, 1972

MANO

White Woman
grinds her grain
on busted cement;

on oil-slick streets
carries her babes,
sometimes forgets
her babes be living.
White Woman
steps to break glass
steps again
to scatter glass
steps again
to watch it go.

White Woman
won't run.
White Woman
grinds her grain
on busted cement.

Berkeley, 1973

there will be
no archaeology
to my bones

my cells will
not forget
how to live
how to be born
how to be still singing
when they feel
the new knowledge
death is

life is dying
each moment
learning to live
each moment
in & out
like bird breath
like toad's tongue
like making love

When I die
I ask only
to be thrown
into the sun.

LONG
DIVISION:
A TRIBAL
HISTORY

Our skin loosely lays
across grass borders;
stones shooting out
are loaded down
with placement sticks,
a great tearing
and appearance of holes.
We are bought and divided
into clay pots; we die
on granite scaffolding
on the shape of the Sierras
and lie down with lips open
thrusting songs on the world.
Who are we and do we still live?
The doctor, asleep, says no.
So outside of eternity
we struggle until our blood
has spread off our bodies
and frayed the sunset edges.
It's our blood that gives you
those southwestern skies.
Year after year we give,
harpooned with hope
only to fall bouncing
through the canyons,
our songs decreasing
with distance.
I suckle coyotes and grieve.

It is I in the cities, in the bars,
in the dustless reaches of cold eyes
who vanishes, who leans underbalanced

into nothing; it is I
without learning, I without song
who dies & cries the death-time

who blows from place to place on creosote dust,
dying over & over. It is I who had to search
& turn the stones, half-dead crawl

through the bones, let tears dissolve in dry caves
where women's ghosts roll *piki**
& insects move to keep this world alive.

It is I who hold the generous bowl
that flows over with shell & stone
& buries its future in blood, places its shape

within rock wall carvings. It is I who die
bearing cracked turquoise & making noise
so as to protect your fragile immortality,

O medicine ones.

piki: rolled-up corn wafers

THE PARTS OF A POET

Loving

the pottery goodness
of my body
    settled down on flowers,
    pulling pollen in great
    handfuls; full & ready

    parts of me are pinned
    to earth, parts of me
    undermine song, parts
    of me spread on the water,
    parts of me form a rainbow
    bridge, parts of me follow
    the sandfish, parts of me
    are a woman who judges.

Falling through the years
like dandelion dust or turquoise
chipped from the matrix and flying,
I am set in troubled silver.
I know there's a first time
for everything, even closed words,
even a finishing. My songs seem undone
when they stomp-dance naked in the moonlight
but children peeping from under dark porches
laugh all the ups and downs in together.

I'll take my old age early
and watch them play
my poems into cat's-cradles.

LOST COPPER

LOST COPPER

Time to tend the fields again
where I laid my bone-handled spade to earth
and dug from its dirt the shy child-songs
that made my mouth a Hopi volcano.
My hands retreat dusty and brown
there being no water pure enough
to slide the ages and stones from my skin,
there being no voice strong enough
to vibrate the skin and muscle apart.
Like a summer-nude horse I roll on my back
and fishtail my hips from side to side;
then on my belly, my navel gone home,
I scrape my cheek and teeth and ride.
From there I rise of earth and wind
to the height of one woman
and cup my breast to the hollow-gourd vine
to feed the place that has sent me songs
to grow from the ground that bears me:
this then my harvest

                    squash-brown daughter
                    blue corn pollen
                    lost copper

No longer the drifting
and falling of wind,
your songs have changed;
they have become
thin willow whispers
that take us by the ankle
and tangle us up
with red mesa stone,
that keep us turned
to the round sky,
that follow us down
to Winslow, to Sherman,
to Oakland, to all the spokes
that leave Earth's middle.
You have engraved yourself
with holy signs, encased yourself
in pumice, hammered on my bones
till you could no longer hear
the howl of the missions
slipping screams through your silence,
dropping dreams from your wings.

        Is this why
        you made me
        sing and weep
        for you?

Like butterflies
made to grow another way
this woman is chiseled
on the face of your world.

The badger-claw of her father
shows slightly in the stone
burrowed from her sight,
facing west from home.

I EXPECTED MY SKIN AND MY BLOOD TO RIPEN

When the blizzard subsided four days later [after the
massacre in 1890 at Wounded Knee], a burial party was
sent . . . a long trench was dug. Many of the bodies were
stripped by whites who went out in order to get the Ghost
shirts and other accoutrements the Indians wore . . . the
frozen bodies were thrown into the trench stiff and naked. . .
only a handful of items remain in private hands . . .
exposure to snow has stiffened the leggings and moccasins,
and all the objects show the effects of age and long use . . .
[items pictured for sale] moccasins $140; hide scraper $350;
buckskin shirt $1200; womens' leggings $275; bone
breastplate $1000. . .

—Kenneth Canfield's 1977 Plains Indian
Art Auction Catalog

I expected my skin and my blood
to ripen, not be ripped from my bones;
like fallen fruit I am peeled, tasted,
discarded. My seeds open
and have no future.
Now there has been no past.
My own body gave up the beads,
my own hands gave the babies away
to be strung on bayonets,
to be counted one by one
like rosary stones and then
tossed to the side of life
as if the pain of their birthing
had never been.
My feet were frozen to the leather,
pried apart, left behind—bits of flesh
on the moccasins, bits of paper deerhide
on the bones. My back was stripped

18

of its cover, its quilling intact,
was torn, was taken away.
My leggings were taken like in a rape
and shriveled to the size
of stick figures
like they had never felt the push
of my strong woman's body
walking in the hills.
It was my own baby
whose cradleboard I held—
would've put her in my mouth like a snake
if I could, would've turned her into a bush
or rock if there'd been magic enough
to work such changes. Not enough magic
to stop the bullets, not enough magic
to stop the scientists, not enough magic
to stop the money.

THREE THOUSAND DOLLAR DEATH SONG

Nineteen American Indian skeletons from Nevada . . .
valued at $3,000.
                    —*invoice received at a museum*
                    as normal business, 1975

Is it in cold hard cash? the kind
that dusts the insides of mens' pockets
laying silver-polished surface along the cloth.
Or in bills? papering the wallets of they
who thread the night with dark words. Or
checks? paper promises weighing the same
as words spoken once on the other side
of the mown grass and dammed rivers
of history. However it goes, it goes.
Through my body it goes
assessing each nerve, running its edges
along my arteries, planning ahead
for whose hands will rip me
into pieces of dusty red paper,
whose hands will smooth or smatter me
into traces of rubble. Invoiced now
it's official how our bones are valued
that stretch out pointing to sunrise
or are flexed into one last fetal bend,
that are removed and tossed about,
cataloged, numbered with black ink
on newly-white foreheads.
As we were formed to the white soldier's voice,
so we explode under white students' hands.
Death is a long trail of days
in our fleshless prison.
From this distant point

we watch our bones auctioned
with our careful quillwork,
beaded medicine bundles, even the bridles
of our shot-down horses. You who have priced us,
you who have removed us—at what cost?
What price the pits
where our bones share
a single bit of memory,
how one century has turned
our dead into specimens,
our history into dust,
our survivors into clowns.
Our memory might be catching, you know.
Picture the mortars, the arrowheads, the labrets
shaking off their labels like bears suddenly awake
to find the seasons ended while they slept.
Watch them touch each other, measure reality,
march out the museum door!
Watch as they lift their faces
and smell about for us. Watch our bones rise
to meet them and mount the horses once again!
The cost then will be paid
for our sweetgrass-smelling having-been
in clam-shell beads and steatite, dentalia
and woodpecker scalp, turquoise and copper,
blood and oil, coal and uranium,
children, a universe
of stolen things.

FOR THE WHITE POETS WHO WOULD BE INDIAN

just once
just long enough
to snap up the words
fish-hooked
from our tongues.
You think of us now
when you kneel
on the earth,
turn holy
in a temporary tourism
of our souls.
With words
you paint your faces.
chew your doeskin,
touch breast to tree
as if sharing a mother
were all it takes,
could bring
instant and primal
knowledge.
You think of us only
when your voice
wants for roots,
when you have sat back
on your heels
and become primitive.
You finish your poem
and go back.

INCIDENT AT A HAMBURGER STAND: IOWA CITY

My eyes so soon after sleeping
and without coffee until this moment
stick quick together, the lids grinding
and half open. Already the shoulders
of a construction worker square
and solidify to remind me
'Girl, you are in the midwest now;
keep your place—eyes down—while
I get a good long look
at your fat Indian body
before I go' and then he turned
and said to his friends
'I'll wait outside
where it's not so
crowded' this last while
turning his mouth
to where I was sitting
in the nearly-empty room
and pointing
with his toothpick.
As he said
I kept my head down
hating myself;
beaded ear-rings,
good southwestern peyote rope,
blasted along
the red of my cheeks.
One last swallow
of creamed coffee
and I tip my head back
to defy him, square up

my own shoulders
and refuse this whiteman's burden.

I am not angry you know
but wonder: what kind of man
can be like that
so early in the morning?

ANOTHER ONE OF THOSE DREAMS
WHERE I GRIND MY OWN COLORS

& bite the basket of this world
inserting filed teeth
between warp & weft
to lift the twining
round its rods
& pull it apart;
undoing my baskets
I take the old bent grasses
& put them to soak, let the reeds
stretch straight again & weave
my wet skin in, twining
moons & arrows into dark designs.
Under my hand is ground
the green mold, the black earth,
the little last touches;
up & down obliquely
my fingers wink in the air
stroking the long reeds with water
pulling about the dust
caught floating
by the first slight circles
of sunrise.

My painted people are orphans; they take me
to earth in great strides and beg for rain;

they are not afraid to strike the sun nor
open the water that seals their throats;

they are rich with pottery dust on their hands,
they are big with the pregnancy of peace;

they shoulder my brushes as I draw them dancing;
they call me mama, they call me orphan.

THE MAN WHO DREAMED HE WAS TURQUOISE

(from a dream by Arthur Murata)

I know the man
who was the form
of turquoise lifted
into air and the man
who knew the artist's
feel, hands that rub
shapes into the form
and surround, search
and find. I know
the man who dreamed
he was turquoise,
laid in matrix,
waiting, following
the artist, finding
the form, chiseling
the night, loving him,
holding him, feeling
of him the red fingers,
peeling of him
along shell and
layers of loam
and the pressing
pounds. I know the man
who was held and
who felt the peeling
away. I know the man
who lay in the mountain
till the artist was born
who would chip and fit,
who would hold, who
would set the form
into sandcast silver,

who would wear the form
in proud dreams.
I know the man
who believed in the man
who would love the form,
who would direct the
forming, who would
contain the form, who
would long for the flow.
I know the man
who knows turquoise
from inside-out,
in a wholeness, who
becomes the shape moving
through the matrix
no different
from a cradle.
I know the man
who found his years
piled up under earth
and felt the earth
shift and change
around him, who laid
with his eyes shut
waiting patiently
for the mines to be
opened. I know the man
who knows the artist
and changes his color
at will, touched and found
between blue and brown.

I know the man
whose fingers bleed
tearing up through
earth; I know the man
who built his strength
bringing turquoise
to the sky. He told me
stones are like this:
bones wrapped in heat
and hardness, rasping
the seasons around
in a gourd and
holding the planet
in place.

WHAT
  HAPPENED
WHEN
  THE HOPI
  HIT
    NEW YORK

1. *From the air*
Islands are green
and blackest black,
the water around them
cobalt; clouds melt
into glaciers that
melt into mountains
and canyons fill silently
with white flesh
waiting.
2. *Islands more islands*
great hands push
water between them
blackening fjords against
the never-setting sun
and placing deep into tongues
the teeth of copper
and caves. Fish become black
on black and spread already
their mouths
as if eager
for the bone hook,
the spear's thrust
and the smoking rack.
3. *Fairbanks*
At some point
during the round day
the blue breath
of the mountain range,
raggedly south, burns
toward July, rehearsing
for a dance that will last

sixty days—resting
from Arctic fevers
and tentative rumbles
and rivers that break
into thousands of arrows,
ice that turns clear then
explodes into mist, valleys
that become a fog of insects
floating over the beaver pond
like nets and the frantic clicking
of round aspen leaves
like fragile coins flipping
in the afternoon rain,
the evening breeze.

4. *Fairbanks, 2:00 a.m.*

Brought to the window
by a brilliant flash
not a snowbank stolen home
in June but the Tanana
shining with midnight's
red sun, early summer's
great moon that dances
on the water and turns to platinum
the whole of the Fairbanks basin.
This is a Drum Dance
turning toward town
from a dozen Yukon villages,
a thousand Native throats.

5. *The worst forest fire in a decade*

Smoke settles all afternoon
and toward evening touches
the aspens; the red fog drops

like a great roan horse
its old flanks bending brittle
and groaning down among
the dim streetlights.
Vapor trails recede
in the blue-white sky,
the Chena like a snake
curls about its eggs.
Inside these tightest of bonds
we continue to sweat change,
heat ourselves into water
and dream of future ice
upon which the spirits
will quarrel and dance.
Southeast, low mountains
grip the sun
to blur summer's smoke
along breaking highways
and the silver pipeline
covered with graffiti and blood.
Old women are leaving
the villages now.
Men bring out
their hatchets and shovels,
prepare the way back
to winter and to home.
6. *Returning south from the air—over Ketchikan*
A long look back:
the sun is sloughing
its salmon skin
along the northernmost

horizon, a line so thin
that it steps through the dark
like a seal slips through water.
And what remains? dissolving touch,
echo of whispers
begun long ago
but kept into summer
remaining to melt
                    smaller and
                    smaller into
                    the sea.

LITERARY LUNCHEON: IOWA CITY

According to the windows
that face the slow-spilling brown river
we are sipping not our coffee
but blizzard winds that surprise us
rolling from the north.
Still-bare trees
are slowly colored white
and the earth implies
this
is the source
of the cold I feel.
Not so.
The great ones gather
at the university buffet
like cattle around
alfalfa and barley.
I maintain
without willing it
an Indian invisibility.

CHICAGO

is a mystery to me
for it does not extend
beyond the foodless corridors
of O'Hare Airport yet
does bring out
the foreigner in me
feeling her way
along the ground
touching ice and earth,
determining existence,
and mapping a path
from west to east
and back again.
All the many things
I've heard about Chicago
narrow into the frame
of this hour: yellow light
slanting across the smoke,
hands groping
toward what is hoped
is a real coffee pot,
lights whirling
and spinning
the planes
to earth,
alien promises
served on toothpicks
in the cocktails.
Ojibwa songs
from behind
the jukebox.

Astonished by what I am breathing—
white water and cobblestones
polished gray by northern feet—
a tourist, I try to figure out the French
on menu after menu, my tongue exhausted
in this southern November. I am listening
for shouts from yesterday
that quickly turn to mist
and to the Gulf dissipate
through the silence of blue shale,
through the solid silk of the Mississippi,
through the sun in slivers against powder
left from mountains dynamited
into the streets
a century ago.
What voice attempted the idiot jump?
What words strangled
or justice quit? By the silence of petroglyphs,
stiff birds and stick women, I am answered.
In an alligator mist they respond
with the rattle of ravens rending flesh,
the sheep scapula scraping
my dry and exposed ribs.
That old enemy song
is hard against my fist.
I choose once more
to walk where native rain slow-boils
and simmers in the true colors
of noon.

MY RED ANTENNAE RECEIVING:
VERMONT

The first thing they said on the day I arrived was,
"We have no Indians here."

Here, too, the skin has been red
and the hands have frozen into wolverine feet
that bend me into a welcoming gesture
through a distance that echoes with death.

Mountain to mountain (none of them so thin
as those I know in the west) sound is cupped
in the earth to erupt another time
when memory begins to edge away.

The voices have no end.
They are not stilled.
Songs steam, dipping into snow
as they look for familiar trails,

for tracks left by ancient tongues,
forgotten women and the places
they propped
their burden baskets.

CORN-GRINDING SONG TO SEND ME HOME:
NEW HAMPSHIRE

Comparing kinds of desert:
    birch and snow bump on my eyes
    like drumbeats, shake me down
    into my shoes like joshua trees
    and dunes never did.
The mountains of the east
are softened and calmed by snow
not angry or chastised
like the temper of the Sierras.
    Rock is made invisible and weak
    letting weasels be tracked
    by the warmth of their scat
    slips of steam as evening comes on.
I am trying this new song with open mouth
yet it catches against my teeth
for something here is different,
is trying to change me
into a shadow disguised
behind closed swollen eyes,
black hair and distorted lips
of a False-face mask.
    My hands are still Hopi
    and will keep me home
    moving back and forth
    palms down, fingers curled
    on cool stone, dreaming
    the metate and maize within.

CEMETERY:
STRATFORD, CONNECTICUT

I am accustomed
with my western eyes
to extremes: the very ancient
or things new enough
to smell like carpet glue.
Like that I have balanced my bones
between the petroglyph
and the mobile home.

I know that what ages earth
has little to do
with things we build
to wrinkle her skin
and fade her eyes-
this for instance

> horizontal tenement
> like the South Bronx
> but flower-infested
> at the end of winter.
> Women cover themselves
> with bright colors
> turning hot
> against the snow,
> stroll slowly
> among ancestors
> labeled and stacked,
> yet afraid to leave
> what they did not build

> the genuine
> earth.

SUBWAY GRAFFITI:
AN ANTHROPOLOGIST'S IMPRESSIONS

New York City, 1978

1.

Day-glo signs of survival
in impossible places
the City
and we primates
consider our position
with full-armed pitches
through the holes
in our future.
We have not been here long enough
to know if there's a reason
to mate. We may be extinct now
as we tunnel through rock,
crush cockroaches
whose record is stronger
and longer than ours.
  Words on subway walls were cries of help
  arrangements made
  treaties abandoned
  death threats
  turned into rumbles
  with name and number
  recorded.
Art starts
pragmatic
becomes design
    dies
    unseen.

2.

My California-born senses
feel the subway
as an earthquake
strangely regular;
I grip the seat
and wait to see
if I should stand
in a doorway or duck
under a table.
 Reality is changed
 from three thousand miles.
 About this earthquake writing:
 fifty feet into island rock
 the people rumbled
 into each other,
dueling for power.
The slippery cliff walls
tell of war, of prayer,
of hunts long over
into the night, of idleness,
of romance, of dripping water,
of scurrying rats, of fires
generating on the ties
and dying, of logical regular
metal-slick strokes
returning through evolution
to basics.
 I can't read most of it.
 Style is now design
 and the messages remain

secret, hieroglyph
not hieratic.

Manhattan has no Rosetta Stone
in the earth to be found
and deciphered
by my probing
colonial tongue.
Train by train,
station by station,
they are
an underground blur.

3.

$$$$ Hunger, engraved shells
    that will feed the deer
    who shelter in my belly.
    I will give you the ocean currents
    if you will salt my rotting meat.
    I will kill the rabbit for you
    if you will make it warm my feet.
    I worship what I kill
    I worship what I eat
    I worship what it means
F— M.A.E. A blow for mankind
    upon womankind.
    From the bruises on your flesh
    you will give me a son.
    With the hand that wrestles
    a digging stick to earth
    you will grasp and I will dig
    all the deeper with my seed.

The weak are to be run over
by my rod of power;
always we must know who is stronger
by the broken bones of my women
and my boys.
DUKES RULE! Our leaders
        eat themselves bare.
        They will not plant,
        they will not hunt.
        They are wasteful
        yet they sharpen their tongues
        on my labor. Not they
        but something greater
        keeps peace in the village
        or lets it go.
        These ones trade wives for manioc.
        macaw feathers for turquoise;
        their power is bound to flesh
        and they are always
        always hungry.
STRIKE!   Obsidian breaks
        under elk antler.
        Flakes, fingernail-shaped,
        spin to my feet.
        This is shaping,
        this is ruling, this is eating,
        this is organizing, this is symmetry,
        this is god, this is copulating
        this is real, this is to be defined,
        this is beyond description.

We will defy
what we need
and we will be the shapers.
SCORE   Our language is precious.
These signs mark our clans
as we are dried
from where we emerged
to this place chosen for us.
We speak, we watch, we sing for signs.
We torment, we tease,
we will not let you hear the words
for they are sacred.
This is who we are;
we are the words.
You may someday hurt us
with the parts left behind,
words that were left
vibrating on the ground,
parings of hair, toenail,
spirit and song.

THE
HALFBREED
CHRONICLES

LOO-WIT*

The way they do
this old woman
no longer cares
what others think
but spits her black tobacco
any which way
stretching full length
from her bumpy bed.
Finally up
she sprinkles
ashes on the snow,
cold buttes
promising nothing
but the walk
of winter.
Centuries of cedar
have bound her
to earth,
huckleberry ropes
lay prickly
on her neck.
Around her
machinery growls,
snarls and ploughs
great patches
of her skin.
She crouches
in the north,

*Loo-Wit: the Cowlitz Indian name for Mount St. Helens in Washington

her trembling
the source
of dawn.
Light appears
with the shudder
of her slopes,
the movement
of her arm.
Blackberries unravel,
stones dislodge.
It's not as if
they weren't warned.

She was sleeping
but she heard
the boot scrape,
the creaking floor,
felt the pull of the blanket
from her thin shoulder.
With one free hand
she finds her weapons
and raises them high;
clearing the twigs
from her throat
she sings, she sings,
shaking the sky
like a blanket about her
Loo-Wit sings and sings and sings!

THROAT SONG: THE WHIRLING EARTH

*Eskimo throat-singers imitate the sounds the women
hear . . . listening to the sound of wind going through the
cracks of an igloo . . . the sound of the sea shore, a river of
geese, the sound of the northern lights while the lights are
coming closer . . . in the old days the people used to think the
world was flat, but when they learned the world was
turning, they made a throat-singing song about it.*

—*Inuktitut Magazine, December 1980*

I always knew you were singing!

As my fingers have pulled your clay,
as your mountains have pulled the clay of me,

as my knees have deeply printed your mud,
as your winds have drawn me down and dried the mud of me,

around me always the drone and scrape of stone,
small movements atom by atom I heard like tiny drums,

I heard flutes and reeds that whine in the wind,
the bongo scratch of beetles in redwood bark,

the constant rattle that made
of this land a great gourd!

O I always knew you were singing!

TRUGANINNY

*Truganinny, the last of the Tasmanians, had seen the stuffed
and mounted body of her husband, and it was her dying
wish that she be buried in the outback or at sea for she did
not wish her body to be subjected to the same indignities.
Upon her death she was nevertheless stuffed and mounted
and put on display for over eighty years.*

— *Paul Coe, indigenous Australian activist, 1972*

You will need
to come closer
for little is left
of this tongue
and what I am saying
is important.

I am
the last one.

I whose nipples
wept white mist
and saw so many
dead daughters
their mouths empty and round
their breathing stopped
their eyes gone gray.

Take my hand
black into black
as yellow clay
is a slow melt
into grass gold
of earth

and I am melting
back to the Dream.

Do not leave
for I would speak,
I would sing
another song.

They will take me.
Already they come;
even as I breathe
they are waiting for me
to finish
my dying.

We old ones
take such
a long time.

Please
take my body
to the source of night,
to the great black desert
where Dreaming was born.
Put me under the bulk
of a mountain
or in
the distant sea.

Put me where
they will not
find me.

THE DAY THEY CLEANED UP THE BORDER:
EL SALVADOR

Government soldiers killed my children. I saw it.
Then I saw the head of a baby floating in the water.

—survivor, El Salvador, 1981

How comforting
the clarity
of water,
flute music
in a rush
or startling hush,
crackle of grass
like seeds
in a gourd
and the soothing whisper
of the reeds.
I prayed
the whole night
to be taken
to my past
for the pounding of rifles
comes again and again
morning by morning
til my two babies lay
with names stolen away
in their beds
and on the ground
where they played.
So many gone
and I prayed
to be taken
for the lizards

to notice and begin
eating at my feet,
work their way up
til even my heart
is nibbled away.
I have come
so many mornings
to the stream,
so many times prayed
in the glistening mist
and now drink oceans
to drown myself
from the mountains
of memory.

But look—that little melon rind
or round gourd, brown and white
in the water where I
could pluck it out
and use it dry, slipping
past me in the ripples
and turning
til its tiny mouth
still suckling
points at me.

ROBERT

*I am death, the destroyer of worlds . . . the physicists have
known sin and this is a knowledge they cannot lose.*

        —*J. Robert Oppenheimer, 1945*

the lines of your arteries
begin to glow making maps
finger follows afraid &
firm pale like the alamagordo sky
the white lizards in the sand

are you humming or is it
a wayward insect or the tremble
of your deepest bones. los alamos
trinity alamagordo (frail robert)
jornada del muerto   you crouch
in the bunker hands to yours eyes
your light gray business suit porkpie hat
loosened tie speaking to
transparent friends or to no one
in particular
it's amazing
how the tools, the technology
trap one
  & you are amazed at the welts
  so wide on your wrists, those chains
  enormous from your belt.
  not even your wife was awake
  morning pivot of your life
  the radio groaned you twisted
  the knob feeling for
  an end to feeling but the voice
  said anyway how your kids went screaming

from the crotch of the plane
mouth-first onto play yard & roof top
& garden & temple, onto hair & flesh
onto steel & clay   leaving you
leaving you   leaving you
your own fingerprints   in the ashes
your vomit   your tears

JULIA

*Julia Pastrana was a mid-19th century singer and dancer in
the circus who was billed as "The World's Ugliest Woman"
or, sometimes, "Lion Lady" because of the long hair
growing on her face and the rest of her body. She was a
Mexican Indian who had been born with facial deformities.
In an effort to maintain control over her professional life, her
manager persuaded her to marry him and she expressed her
belief that he was in love with her. She bore a son who
inherited her physical abnormalities but only lived for six
hours. She died three days later. Her husband, unwilling to
forfeit his financial investment, had Julia and her infant boy
stuffed, mounted and put on display together in a glass case.
Their location is currently unknown, but they have been
displayed in the United States and Europe as recently as
1975. Her husband died in an asylum.*

Tell me it was just a dream,
my husband, a clever trick
made by some tin-faced village god
or ghost coyote, to frighten me
with his claim that our marriage is made
of malice and money.
O tell me again
how you admire my hands,
how my jasmine tea is rich and strong,
my singing sweet, my eyes so dark
you would lose yourself swimming
man into fish
as you mapped the pond
you would own.
That was not all.
The room grew cold
as if to joke

with these warm days;
the curtains blew out
and fell back against
the moon-painted sill.
I rose from my bed like a spirit
and, not a spirit at all, floated slowly
to my great glass oval
to see myself reflected
as the burnished bronze woman
skin smooth and tender
I know myself to be
in the dark
above the confusion
of French perfumes
and I was there in the mirror
and I was not.

I had become hard
as the temple stones of Ótomi,
hair grown over my ancient face
black moss, gray as jungle fog
soaking green the tallest tree tops.
I was frail
as the breaking dry branches
of my winter sand canyons,
standing so still
as if to stand forever.

O such a small room!
No bigger than my elbows
outstretched
and just as tall
as my head.

A small room from which
to sing open the doors
with my cold graceful mouth,
my rigid lips, my silence
dead as yesterday,
cruel as the children
and cold as the coins that glitter
in your pink fist.
And another magic
in the cold
of that small room:
in my arms or standing
next to me on a tall table
by my right side
a tiny doll
that looked
like me.

O my husband
tell me again
this is only a dream
I wake from warm
and today is still today,
summer sun and quick rain;
tell me, husband,
how you love me
for my self
one more time.

It scares me so
to be with child,
lioness
with cub.

WHAT
    THE MOHAWK
MADE
   THE HOPI
      SAY

The volume from which this section comes was a collaboration with my traveling partner, Maurice Kenny.

LENAPE

Baltimore, 1984

The shaggy winter birches of Virginia
do not hide your movement,
you thin and wailing mouth
among the rusted red bud
candle-flame faces,
the tiny farms, the gravel lots,
you, shadow, slipping between
tomcat and tombstone.

All of winter brought me here,
your footprints that glitter
in the grass laying it back
along the bloody ground,
drops of blood—frozen garnets—
guided me to your Longhouse dance.

What brings you back
to bring me here
sipping coffee just now
on the deadly railway?
As if the rain would tell,
its moist fingers
knead my hair.

REMINDER

Baltimore, 1984

The rubble on which you kneel
stumbling from the train
is made of bones, the blackened bones
of coal miners—rib and spine,
the still-white teeth, the wrists
swelling and seething
in the earth.

And the smoke of your singing
bears me back to the train,
takes me north again
in a furious hustle,
embarrassed hush.

Why must you tell me
my bones are not alone,
that there are so many
songs in the ground?

LEAVING PORT AUTHORITY FOR AKWESASNE

New York City, 1985

I saw a mesa
between two buildings,
a row of tall
narrow houses,
bare as the desert I know,
the roofs appearing
in clumps like greasewood.
O Wendy, he said
looking at his fingernails,
that's Weehawken.

One way or another
we'll get somewhere soon
for I have seen crows
dance on Manhattan snow,
a hawk on Henry Street,
smoke plumes from the lips
of street kids,
mesas along the Hudson.

I am getting ready.

WHAT THE MOHAWK MADE THE HOPI SAY

Somewhere in the Adirondacks, January 1985

Unaccustomed to breath
frozen so still
as to crackle
from nose to lip,
I search the birches
for a squirrel's tail jerk,
the roadside pond
for quail or swan.
Or is this that famous sleep
they speak of with fever in the east
or up in the mountains
when the words just yawn
and settle on their hands?

Tell me again
I have no winter at home
and the tongues that lap
against my bones
bear no leaves.
Bless this tongue
in your special way,
make brittle the spit
and faceted the tear,
make diamonds
from my turquoise,
crystal light
to illumine your ice.

I finally agree
turning into a rock
that these are mountains
noble as any
and all of Arizona
must wait
for spring thaw.

SIX NATIONS MUSEUM

Onchiota, New York   *January 1985*

Is this your special light
salmon blushing west to sky
and these your white pines,
your tangled twigs, the brush
of your fingers
through everything
                    tobacco to north
                    tobacco to east
Is this what you mean
by the Eastern Door,
the faces and feet
crowded between
silence of willow,
bare waving hands of redbud,
stark bones of birch
                    tobacco to south
                    tobacco to west
And the moon that waited
within my belly
for the smoking song
to blossom, the wild turkeys
to appear, then gently came
wide open as
the wise women are.
                    tobacco to sky
                    tobacco to earth
                    tobacco to all
                    my relations.

ADIRONDACK TRAILWAYS AS SPIRIT HELPER

(on the bus between Saranac Lake & New York City)

Perhaps it was no accident
that the northbound bus to Massena
froze, preparing our blood
and our breath for the cold
steaming intensity of Akwesasne
and later
                    that the southbound bus
to New York City kept us walking
hot among remembered wampum,*
and ladled water to white-hot stones
to leach the last bit
of hurry from our bones

wampum: Contrary to non-Native American folklore, wampum is not
money. It is a form of literature, written in clamshell beads, that can be read
at important events. It resembles the Congressional Record far more than
it resembles money or jewels.

GOING
TO WAR
WITH ALL
MY
RELATIONS

WHAT DISTINGUISHES SUNSET IN SEATTLE
FROM SUNSET IN CHICAGO

is that bristling flesh on the blue horizon,
muscled grizzly hump and forest of fur
above yellow eyes, or Her
> though her blanket rips more each year
> and her gray hair smokes and smolders
> with spruce. Her trembling song we feel
> when we dream too deep. I feel her
and the jet plane
shakes her
visible again.

> *Loo-Wit Baker Mazama Hood*
> *Shasta Lassen Tamalpais Diablo*

Listen to her
wanting to know
if our tongues drip lava,
if our flesh empties itself,
if our hands are hollow.
Or if we have fire inside
as she does
and huddle like her
in the high winter night,
if we know the feel
of the swelling mound
inevitable eruption,
or emergence,
if we know the sight
of snow blackened
the way the wind blows

Mammoth Lake San Andreas
Coalinga
Jump and dance! Jump and
dance!

Old friends blinking in new sun
we take sharp ashes and rub dark the east.
We have become
the distant naked silhouettes
of spirits picking nettles.
We have become ones who are careful
to mend the bowls, sew tight the boots,
waterproof the baskets
with the blood of ourselves

one of us a woman
one of us a raven
one of us an airplane

MARGARET NEUMANN

Born 1832, Darmstadt, Germany. Died 1925, San Francisco.

*—From a 1912 photograph of Margaret holding
her great-granddaughter, Betty, my mother.*

The dangerous dreams of a wild girl,
they said, who goes to meet her husband
beneath the twisting serpent and eagle
of Mexico's flag

      who mounts the wagon bound for California
      where the very streets are gold, gold on which
      stolen kisses fall not gently at all and the
      sun glimmers
      from a thousand Spanish swords, ankle-deep
      already
      in Miwok bones.

Gold the river
that pulled you west,
the tall grass, orange poppies
rising from rock and swamp,
red the Missouri mud
that transformed you
at the border and this now
is mine as you try
to imagine me.

      The rivers Merced and Mokelumne,
      San Joaquin and Fresno,
      feed great pastures of blood
      and secret shining crops—
      Bear Creek blood, blood of
      Mariposa,
      Yosemite blood, Ahwahneechee
      blood,

places made bad
in the night of red water.

            • • •

Emiliana. Elfriede. Lenchen.
Pictures on brittle cardboard
of corseted girls
and their tortoise-shell combs.
Did they see you step onto the boat?
Did they dream shut the sails
and will the wind to die?
Did they think of impaling themselves
as romantic heroines
on the pointed mouth of the ship
or of drowning themselves daintily
in the lapping gray sea?
Did they give one glance back,
one final goodbye, words that must last
a lifetime?

                • • •

Into the muscle and flesh
of what you called wilderness
you drove the brown horses
through skinny bullpines
and crooked white oaks of drought.
You brought to life
the anxious temblor
in my heart.

Are you the astonished one
or am I? that we meet like this
between the sailing ship
and the silver jet
crossing the sky?

More than a century later
my brown hands cannot recall
your Germany or your Mother Lode,
Yosemite untouched by tourists
buying ice cream and souvenirs
in Tenaya's hiding place.
My questions burn
and summon fire
older than the sun.

If you are a part of me
I am also that crazy acorn
within your throat
around which pioneer stories
rattle and squirm.
If you are the brave heritage
of Gold Rush California,
I am also the bone that buzzes
behind your breast.
If I am the tongue made indigenous
by all the men you would love,
I am also the ghost
of the pioneer's future.

Native storms wail.
Death rides the frontier.
I am the other voice
blasted from the mountain
by hydraulic cannons,
the other fetus
embalmed on your knee.

. . .

Touching the silver
at the center of us both
I believe you would understand.
Do you remember
the sacred signs
painted in the startling blue,
spirits that mumbled
in the German Black Forest?
Do you remember the tribes
that so loved their land
before the roll
of Roman wheels?

Albuquerque, 1989

Unable to sit on the earth
that made manhood from
his forefathers' bones,
the whiteman has chiseled
the faces of his dead
on the very bones
of the hill.
And of our own father—
if I comb the wind-cut feathers
from his skull and trap the ancient flesh
of his neck in buttoned collar and tie,
does he become
your father then?
And if his pony stumbles in the sand,
unravels into dust and dies,
and his children fail to recall
that their future was camping
on his tongue, and if his skin
and toenails thin into paper,
does he become for you
finally a man?

The very mountain
withholds its blessing.
Lizards scramble
to re-make its face.

It was a thing to melt the heart of man, if it was of stone, to
see those little children, with their bodies shot to pieces,
thrown naked into the pit . . .

—*observer of mass burial at Wounded*
Knee, South Dakota, December, 1890

O
how I wish your heart
would melt
    do you see
    it was that way
        we became the stones
        that bruised your feet
        on the prairie
        so that every twisted ankle
        and broken wheel
        would remind you
        of the babies in the snow,
        of the blood and wind,
        the empty sky that day
        aching for geese
        or for the world
        to stop trembling
        and remember new seed.
We became
stones
in that way
cradled in the dry wash
and bursting
through yellow sand.

We have learned
to barricade the village
        and have our weapons
        closer at hand.

EXCAVATION AT SANTA BARBARA MISSION

When archaeologists excavated Santa Barbara Mission in
California, they discovered human bones in the adobe walls.

My pointed trowel
is the artist's brush
that will stroke and pry,
uncover and expose
the old mission wall.

How excited I am
for like a dream
I wanted to count myself
among the ancient dead
as a faithful neophyte
resting there and in love
with the padres
and the Spanish hymns.

A feature juts out. Marrow
like lace, piece of a skull,
upturned cup, fingerbones
scattered like corn
and ribs interlaced
like cholla.

So many bones
mixed with the blood
from my own knuckles
that dig and tug
in the yellow dust.

How fragile
they have become
to float and fall
with my touch,

brittle white tips
shivering into mist.
How helpless I am
for the deeper I go
the more I find
crouching in white dust,
listening to the whistle
of longbones breaking
apart like memories.
My hands empty themselves
of old dreams,
drain the future
into the moisture
of my boot prints.
Beneath the flags
of three invaders,
I the hungry scientist
sustaining myself
with bones of
men and women asleep in the wall
who survived in their own way
Spanish swords, Franciscans
and their rosary whips,
who died among the reeds
to wait, communion wafers
upon the ground, too holy
for the priests to find.

They built the mission with dead Indians.
They built the mission with dead Indians.
They built the mission with dead Indians.
They built the mission with dead Indians.

NOTES ON A CONSPIRACY

*Collection of aboriginal Indian skulls exhibited by the
Academy of Natural Sciences of Philadelphia; 44 skulls from
35 tribes found in graves and on battlefields. Many from
extinct tribes . . .*
                                        —*auction catalog, 1977*

I knew those diggers would find a way
to rack the willow twigs of my arms
tied as they were behind shovel-cracked ribs
sticking into the sky where the sand sloughs away.
I wander lost in the antelope's dream
searching for relations beneath each rock,
praying that I will not go to war alone
with eyes open for the great old visions
of cougar and bear, but with rattlesnake
as I pass and listen to her song.

Who would have thought we could be ended?
Betrayal is as real as the acorns in my spine.
Extinction whips overhead in the storm,
a constant threat to the fishbone charms.
The rain-crazy river whirls me
into obsidian fog.
Where skullmongers whisper among themselves and plot,
believing they wrestled long enough with the sea and won,
from their smooth canals they sailed and said
'We deserve to be here. We were destined for this.'
And how little we knew! We should have asked
'Where is the dust of your mothers? Your own land?
Why did you come so far? What sacred gift do you bring?
What of your humor?
All this talk
of money and estates!'

And we. Where is our strength
that was in acorn and bluejay,
tules laughing in the afternoon wind?
When do we dance—you remember the one—
where we bring up the sun with a shout?
They blame us for their guilt.
They say we are a privileged few.
They say we gamble too much—
we who changed faster than anything,
we who gambled with a snap and glimmer
of vanishing light, eclipse of moon.
We who felt our joints twisted apart,
hands forced empty of memory.
We felt our eyes melt from their sockets
as we were spinning away from the world
and now the scientist wonders at the bullet he lifts
from the small soft place where my daughter sleeps.
Look! how like a furious gun he finds himself
drowned in the blood of dead nations!
Look! how he suffocates in his own poisonous air!
He cannot hear the sound
of my teeth in his bucket.
He does not feel the point
of his own probing trowel.

YELLOW RIBBONS

Baghdad vision, 1991

Her useless hands skim along plastic buttons
fastening as fast as she can
but the child comes pouring out
as deep a red as rubies,
makes no sound.

Rubble is no bed.
Bandages loosen and stream from her wrists
like ribbons on the day she married
but the siren wails and the women wail
and old men done with the business of war
raise their faces to heaven,
hard hands flat against their ears.

Grandmother stands on one foot then the other
quietly watches the workers pass
fretting to escape the storm
while men she does not know
pass around the bricks and burnt things
that penetrate her dreams
from the artificial tumbled mountain
that was, last night, her home.

The white hills of the child's own mother
froze on the inner side of his eyelids
as they were watching TV when the lights went out
and a thousand thunders enclosed them.
They touched hand to hand once more
exploding the future from twisted steel.

At least we fought, the patriarch said
heaving the last of his home on his back.
At least we did not die like victims
sucking poison into our lungs

but like warriors of God.
And every younger man trembled
and began to walk the refugee trail.

Tie a yellow ribbon around these.
Tie a yellow ribbon around strong young men
the future of a nation
dancing death postures
as they burn in their tanks.
Tie a yellow ribbon around ragged white flags,
blasted to bits, truth retreating as Sand Creek's ghosts
sit on the memory of black bayonets.
Tie a yellow ribbon around the blood-spattered parade,
around bewildered mothers, lost and weeping elders,
lonely voices that cry and beg for peace.

O yankee fist,
the souvenirs are bleeding.

Fresno, 1991

NOW POOF
SHE IS
GONE

The first seven poems are a selection from Now Poof She Is Gone *forthcoming from Firebrand Press, Ithaca, New York.*

I could no more close my ears to your sound
than bring home the useless bright skin
of murdered serpents, moist ribbons
of transparent beads that stretch
and twist in the wind. But I have done that
a thousand times.
                    Did everyone agree
                    I would come to no good?
                    that men must be tricked
                    into fatherhood?
                    And women destined to whirl away
                    wincing in the storm,
                    daughters crumbling
                    with small hands desperate
                    to cover the scars
                    left moaning
                    on their bones?
Two hundred acres of madrone burst into flame.
Under helicopters that dip & hover like dragonflies,
manzanita explodes from the sudden heat.
Rusted gray bombers push pink semen from their bodies
& trucks rumble past, rounding up the men
who live in the mountains.
From the westernmost point
of the dissolving sky,
the Sierras abandon themselves
turning to red smoke
as the valley
lays into fog.

like a dandelion gone to seed,
leaving nothing behind but a dent
or not even that to touch or burn
or remember. This is the way
winter begins—
　　with the angry moth
　　who grips the window screen
　　and freezes into an opal.
　　Well, that's one way to go—
　　just get harder. Or I could dissolve
　　as disobedient women do in the Bible
　　their solemn salt hands still pointing
　　to the pleasures of sin.
　　I could evaporate or liquify
　　or become dust or turn sideways
　　before a funhouse mirror
　　to become a needle
　　becoming nothing.
I could scream so mightily
that only sound would survive.
I could cry myself dry,
be sifted by the desert wind
that burns my summer gold hills.
Or I could fly apart
　　and watch my whirling blood
　　form galaxies in the air,
　　spatter on the men
　　who hammer to death
　　the trees and remark

         that a woman just
             was standing there
and now
poof she is gone.

Coarsegold, 1991

hands lowered, wind on her back,
brilliant summer sky pressing down?
Will you return with her
to where the ghosts live?
Way back before she forgot
where all the wounds were
or what the weapon looked like,
before the long climb
to anesthesia.
Seeing the ghosts are gone
or changed forever, faded
into the white July haze,
granite becomes granite,
the south wind bears rain,
all the small lizards
are only what they seem.
Permafrost woman melts in the sun.
Her adobe-thick skin and heart sealed tight
from trespass as well as from
the nourishing rain,
she tries to paint away
the lies with white clay,
so exhausted she cannot stop.
This is her very voice,
her medicine,
seized and drained
into the sand.

tough as treebark
riding on my dream
because I was so strong.
The horns that bend
beyond my back
were silver
and silver the place
where bobcat balanced.
They called me
fish out of water.
Not so. The last leaf
on the willow
brave enough to laugh
to the end.

This was the body I was promised
and this was the tree
that rattled dead in the rain.
This was the song I knew they would give me
and this is the foot
that forgot to be graceful.
This is the starving infant hugging the sun
and this is the precious stick
that never gave a damn
about roots.
This is the one sleeping
where sorcery sings
in the forest of anesthesia
where one small smile
may be deafening.

O please give me new words
that will not stutter
against my teeth.

Coarsegold, 1989

She bore no children
but ghosts emerged
from between her legs.

Dare to believe
that roots can be built
like a pot
in ascending circles
and that skin
will just naturally form
copper sheets
on the bones.
Promise
that a name will appear
blazing from the cliff,
that this is a harvest
large enough for life
and her life is not
half empty but has so much
farther to go.
Step Softly.
She is not of this world
and no one rides
to the rescue.

Before the Old Woman of eastern light
comes rubbing the mountain ridge with ochre
I open, a silver moth, and step
through the dying heart.
You, sleeping in the earth, wake up.
Gather and glue your bones
with aboriginal skill.
Pull yourself into the sky,
be like the sun, become whole
and slowly dissolve, dissipate,
wonder what is left of she
who breaks and crumbles
fingers teeth skin bones splitting
from the top down with words
that are vomit and songs
that explode uselessly
in the womb.

HOLODECK

(with apologies to "Star Trek: The Next Generation")

When they come
I go into my head
private holodeck
so easy
     like breathing
and when that room is locked
and I am trapped in the world
it is like when
     the breathing stops.

          Program: ongoing saga
          of voices
          that beg me not to die
          when I am lost
          to forces so great
          so out of control
          it is not just loss
          but tribunal,
          a thing to be worn
          like armband or badge
          so that every face and hand
          stops, knows and agrees, remembers
          there is a reason to grieve.
          Baskets full of regret
          but no one scolds me
          for feeling sorry for myself again.
          I ask everyone to sit and listen.
          The miracle is that they do.

Mesquite   meets gray eagle-tail fan at my back,
    sings red flashes, hangs from thunderclouds, howls
    words that cannot be understood
    except as hooks
    that do a spinning sort of dance.
          Witness the soaring splashes
          of de Grazia wings*
          on Indian babies, sad flicker
          from a thousand invisible votives.
Lava   bubbles deep burgundy, calls back
    to life junipers killed by bulldozers, yucca and lily
    uprooted where joshua tree priests, warriors
    among broken boulders go
    to where a stupid lord will snub them.
Snow   has melted on the leather wings of jimson weed
    lost medicine endlessly circling the skies above limbo.
    The door into darkness waits, ajar, as we play games
    with the guard, trudge home
    with feet made numb, hands made empty.

*de Grazia wings: refers to the painting style of a Southwestern artist

MOISTURE IN THE AIR
STILL FROM YESTERDAY'S STORM

where I stand
on snail's silver trail
shielded from noon
by long minutes of song
and a certainty
that every beginning
will end in this world.
I want to mend spirits
and dream again,
to fly to tomorrow
and dance in my shawl.
I remember how it lifted,
sun-faces looking up,
to watch your monumental tremor,
your shaking mesquite,
sharp yucca quivering in the sky,
scarecrow dancing
on the purple horizon.

PLUTONIUM VESPERS

Fresno, 1987

Grand mother
Grand father

take this offering
of flesh, this color
and this color, take
all the memories,
take the pain,
take it and shake it
everywhere shake it
all of us shaking
I am shaking

I hear you in a whisper
cricket's voice and thunder;
I hear you warble, rasp,
be in the bullroarer
mimicking hummingbird's wings.
I hear you in woodpecker's laugh,
the creaking wood floor,
silent swift dive of bat;
I hear you in the bending reeds,
brittle oak leaves, the furry moss.

Pity these ones, pity them,
pity these ones, pity the skin
that hangs in ribbons, pity
the round eyes, melted tongue,
pity the sunlight stolen,
white grass uncoiling underground;
pity these ones
who have been touched
by untouchable stuff.

Pity them in the fearsome rain,
pity them who shit great bombs onto earth,
pity the woman who stepped
on the serpent,
pity the quivering sky, the stars
of the milky way, creation
as it unravels, pity us shaking

this small offering is for you,
this small thing, black
willow stick, smoldering sage,
granite crumbling into sand,
the wayward bug, the scorched bone,
for you
Grandmother
Grandfather

*This is the true story of the disappearance of Osceola's head
as given to us by our grandfather. After the death of the
Seminole chief, Dr. Weedon was able to be alone with the
body. During this time he cut off the head, but left it in the
coffin with the scarf that Osceola habitually wore tied as
usual around the neck. Not long before the funeral, Dr.
Weedon removed the head . . . Dr. Weedon took the head
back to St. Augustine with him, and kept it in his home on
Bridge Street, where he also had his office . . . doctors then
thought nothing of collecting heads of savage tribesmen . . .
Dr. Weedon was an unusual man, and his methods of child
training would not find favor today, for he used to hang the
head of Osceola on the bedstead where his three little boys
slept, and leave it there all night as punishment . . .*

—May McNeer Ward [Dr. Weedon's great-granddaughter],
Florida Historical Quarterly 33, nos. 3 & 4, 1955

We remember something
closing around our necks
inevitable as insects
and tricky as the swamp.
We speak to the perpetrator
or risk becoming him,
killer of coral snakes,
blind invader of coffins,
but we have learned
to keep our heads
and never forget
how it was
in the grave.

O yes we became the dust
settled on your hearts.
We became the twin deer
dancing on delicate hooves.
We became the whirlpool
stealing all the books.
We became peaches
bursting through
the end of summer.
We became
all of the murders
returning
We
became whole again.

Okemah, Oklahoma, June 1985

COYOTE

(for Ines & Fred)

That he goes on all fours
should not confuse you
nor that he marks his scent
on cedar and barks his bark
at a broken moon. Suspended
from the stars, we try to listen
but you have to understand
that when he leaps between your knees
chews up your shirt
and pisses in your mouth,
that is only his way.
That is just who he is.
When he mocks your panic,
brush it off. Never mind
that he howls at your pain.
If you sweat in terror
at his reckless career
when he is the murderous driver
at the wheel
and you are the rabbit
trembling on the road,
remember who he is
It explains everything.

Acknowledgments

The author gratefully acknowledges permission to reprint
poems from her previously published collections:

Hopi Roadrunner Dancing (Greenfield Review Press, 1973).
Long Division: A Tribal History (Strawberry Press, 1976. Reprint 1982).
Lost Copper (Malki Museum Publications, 1980. Reprint 1992).
What Happened When the Hopi Hit New York (Contact II Publications, 1982).
The Halfbreed Chronicles & Other Poems (West End Press, 1985. Reprint 1992).
Going to War with All My Relations (Northland Publishers, 1993).
What the Mohawk Made the Hopi Say (Strawberry Press, 1993).

In addition to the above collections, the author wishes to thank the
editors of the following anthologies and periodicals for permission to
reprint the following poems:

Time to Greez (Glide Publications, 1975) for "Lab Genesis" and "Mano."
Alcaeus Review for "Lab Genesis."
Kenyon Review for "Remember waking up with me" and "Do you see
   her on the Mountain."
BOUNDARY 2 for "Retrieving Osceola's Head."

The poems "Dry Lightning," "Is it crazy to want to unravel," "Remem-
ber waking up with me," "Do you see her alone on the mountain,"
"Forty, Trembling," and "Coarsegold Morning" are scheduled for
publication in a new collection entitled *Now Poof She Is Gone* (Firebrand
Press, Fall 1994).

About the Author

Wendy Rose has twice been nominated for the Pulitzer Prize in poetry. She has authored eight volumes of poetry, and her work has appeared in numerous anthologies. Since 1984 she has been the coordinator and an instructor of American Indian Studies at Fresno City College. Her tribal affiliations are Hopi and Miwok.